Meaningful Business

Meaningful Business

a midrash

❁

James M. Houston

REGENT COLLEGE PUBLISHING
Vancouver, British Columbia

Regent College Publishing
5800 University Boulevard
Vancouver, BC V6T 2E4 Canada
www.regentpublishing.com

Regent College Publishing is an imprint of the Regent Bookstore <www.regentbookstore.com>. Views expressed in works published by Regent College Publishing are those of the author and do not necessarily represent the official position of Regent College <www.regent-college.edu>.

ISBN 978-1-57383-535-0

Cataloguing in Publication information is available from Library and Archives Canada.

Contents

Preface

This book is a Christian companion to the book my son, Christopher Houston, has published, titled *For Goodness' Sake*, which was written for a secular readership. Our purpose is for Christian business executives to communicate and enact business ethics with a Christian ethos while being personally edified to know the biblical principles that lie behind all good business practice. The questions at the end of each chapter of Meaningful Business are intended for study groups, perhaps meeting on a regular basis, to encourage one another as business leaders. I am grateful to Jordan Pinches for his editorial assistance in the completion of the text. You may find the original text upon which this commentary is based at Telosity.net.

Introduction

The Incarnation, as all Christians will attest, was the most momentous change in world history, authenticated as occurring "in the reign of Caesar Augustus, when the first census took place while Quirinius was Governor of Syria", as written by a Roman physician and historian, Luke, in his gospel account (Chapter 2:1-2). Ever since the Incarnation, immanence and transcendence have been inseparable, which in business is illustrated by what one rogue trader, or innocent bank official can do, with a computer and the flick of a key, to create even the crash of the whole banking institution.

In life and in business, we never know what small details can have such a magnitude of consequences. The Gospels likewise record minute details like a lad "with five small barley loaves and two small fishes" (John 6: 9), or "Peter's catch of 153 large fish" as recorded in John 21:11. Yet it is John who portrays the overwhelming transcendence of the Eternal Logos becoming a man. (John 1:1-4).

Similar to the young lad in John chapter 6, Chris and I bring to the Lord these small barley loaves and fishes with the hope that He might use them to encourage and sustain you on your journey. As father and son, Chris and I are in a loving complement. We each have unique perspective and experience, that, after years of divergence, have intersected here. In some ways, this course and work is a coming together that has been borne out over two lifetimes, rich and varied. One of us served first as a fisheries ecologist in the interior of British Columbia, working with others to pioneer the repair of ecosystems still underway, and then later to come alongside leaders in some of the whales of business, serving as a management consultant. The other trained as a geographer, helping to pioneer regional planning in war-time Scotland, only to later enter the incipient discipline of the history of ideas, and spiritual theology, ultimately to take part in a new regional plan the Lord had for the Christian landscape here in Vancouver.

Each narrative, distinct yet complementary, can be used in extraordinary and unexpected ways in the hands of the Lord. In service to Him, nothing is wasted.

How wonderful it is to serve our Lord in the places to which he calls us! Together, Chris and I hope our life-time experiences, shared in part here with you, will be helpful and encouraging to you as a Christian taking up the Lord's call to lead in business today.

Midrash, as you may know, was an early genre of rabbinic commentary on the Torah. This is a similar attempt to comment on a text, add colour and highlight meaning for a particular audience. In this case, the audience are Christians, but the text, a short book for leaders in business entitled *For Goodness' Sake: Satisfy the hunger for meaningful business*, is by no means scripture! However, the concept of *midrash* is a helpful one for what this short companion text will attempt to do. Assuming you have already discovered and read the foundational text, let us begin.

Commons and Panarchy

In nature we have bio-diversity, of which mono-culture becomes wholly destructive. This is worst in the Tropics where bio-diversity is greatest. Little do most of us realize that such tropical imbalance can throw the whole realm of bio-diversity into chaos, as the northward advance of giant ants is occurring into the northern hemisphere, having a massiveness that could overwhelm all other living species. Likewise, emotional balance is such a crucial necessity for life sustainability and for healthy human relationships.

When five billionaires equal the wealth of over 6.3 million of the poorest human beings, we are witnessing what huge global economic imbalances can occur.

Pursuing economic balance, or in other words, care and concern for people who are poor is a primary Biblical principle for socio-economic sustainability. "When you gather the harvest of your land, do not reap to the very edges of your field or gather the gleanings of your harvest. Do not go over your vineyard a second time, or pick up the grapes that have fallen. Leave them for the poor and

the foreigner, i.e. the homeless. I am the Lord your God".
(Leviticus 19:9-10)

At a more profound sense, we have the great challenge: "What shall it profit a man if he gain the whole world and lose his own soul". The catastrophic dehumanization of the Industrial Revolution added further momentum to what the slave-trade had done beforehand, that is to think of humans as 'things'. It is a theme the social critic Charles Dickens was to depict in the midst of the sudden acquirement of wealth in the English Industrial Revolution. Yet clearly the message is being less and less heeded by some. Thankfully, we do see the wonderful changes in the creative and generous imagination of some global philanthropists who suggest that economic prosperity must be sustained by more economic justice.

It has also been pointed out that the principle of *panarchy* operates at the level of personal health. Obsession with fear drives one to be distracted by a pleasure principle, be it sex, alcohol, or drugs. Quickly one becomes addicted, only to become aware as Diogenes rebuked his student Alexander the Great, that he had become his own worst enemy. The greatest military commander of the ancient world destroyed himself at age 32, likely as a result of his inability to control his drinking. Too many ambitious business executives are destroying themselves by stress related diseases, precisely because they have become too ambitious, or too fearful to draw reasonable boundaries for their work load, or too emotionally insecure in not delegating to others. Emotional balance is such a crucial necessity for life sustainability and for healthy human relationships.

The Panarchy Principle

The meaning of the word is derived from *Pan,* the unpredictable, universal god of Nature. Pan was the controller and arranger of the four elements – earth, water, air, and fire – and therefore marshalled an all-pervasive, spiritual power, creative and destructive, who both de-stabilizes and sustains, paradoxically. Our description of the emotion *panic* comes from these same roots. Similarly, these are the inherent features of *panarchy.*[1]

It is a logical step to develop a nascent theory of regional sustainability that integrates ecologic, economic, and social dynamics. This brings together resource conservation, business development, and community empowerment objectives. Naturally, any one of the elements in this triad dominating the others would be self-destructive. Neither 100 per cent conservation, nor 100 per cent business development, nor 100 per cent community empowerment would do, but rather the balance of the three which is optimal. But it is significant that culturally the three should have arisen together, in the early 1930's, in the aftermath of the financial crash of 1929. In the hungry years that followed, community empowerment devel-

1. Lance H. Gunderson, C.S. Holling, edit., *Panarchy: Understanding Transformations in Human and Natural Systems* (Washington DC: Island Press, 2002).

oped, yet also early "systems thinking" began to take into account ecology and ecosystems more broadly.

However, there is a limit to each of these systems of equilibrium, such as when ecologists limit their understanding and propose inadequate actions by largely ignoring human behavior, or other organizational structures, or institutional arrangements, that all attempt to mediate the relationships between people and nature.

An ecosystem may be defined as places on earth that consist of both biotic components (life) and abiotic or physical components.[2] These components interact in such a way that a dynamic set of processes produces a complex and diverse set of structures. Space and time are critical dimensions, providing the basis from which theory can be generated and hypothesis can be tested. The scale of ecosystems is as wide as the Pacific Ocean, or as small as a patch in a forest, or a few rocks perched on a mountain summit. Likewise, the time scale can be as vast as climate change, or as finite as an unusual warm afternoon.

A social system is defined by a group of people who interact long enough to create a shared set of understandings, norms, or routines, to integrate action, and to establish patterns of behavior, dominant or submissive.[3] It may be as small as a family, or as large as a neighborhood, a small or a large business. Time scales of response are appropriate to the character of the disturbance, as well as to

2. R.S. Carpenter, "Ecosystem Ecology", in *Ecology*, edit. S. I. Dodson, *et al* (New York: Oxford University Press, 1998), pp. 119-38.
3. Gunderson and Holling, *op. cit.*, pp. 103-119.

the frequency of the disturbances. People's personalities, their admixture of emotions, cognitive thought, and intensity of spirit, are all in the hopper, too! How involved do we get, or how abstract or distanced do we remain, from other people? Such the risk of devolving into *panarchy* can be applied to all human reality, and to all our experience of being alive! Yet we do so cautiously, for people are not just ecosystems. For in addition to space and time being the dimensions of ecosystems, there is a third dimension with people, symbolic construction or meaning.[4]

Of course, the Christian in business has the richest of all experience to draw upon in avoiding the perils of *panarchy* - for we are alive before the Trinitarian God – our God who is consubstantiated as Father, Son, and Holy Ghost.

And yet, living in the post-modern world, we daily see the consequences of ignoring this principle of panarchy. We see it in our emphasis on logic and the hyper-cognitive self, precipitating "the Malaise of Modernity," as Charles Taylor has famously described the change since the 1960's.[5] Unilateralism will always fail, whether it be rationalism, emotionalism, or psychologism. Every "-ism" absolutizes an unsustainable territory. So, in response, we must always seek and explore balance, which seems to often manifest in triadic relationships, whether body, mind, and spirit; or space, time, and life; or even in the disci-

4. *Ibid,* p. 119.

5. Charles Taylor, *The Malaise of Modernity* (CBC Massey Lectures, Toronto, 1991).

plines of ecology, economy, and sociology, which are best understood in relation to one another.

Panarchy in the Kingdom of God

In the evolution of religion, it is curious how indigenous people in the remote ethnic groups of the Himalayan mountains believed in three gods, just as the Shoguns who parade the streets of Japanese communities in May still do, with three distinct tabernacles for their three gods. The Nagas, a buffer state between India and China, rapidly became "Christianized" because the smart Texan Baptist missionaries at the beginning of the 20th century could name the three gods, as Father, Son, and Holy Spirit! These primitive peoples were dimly aware for millennia that triadic relations existed in their cosmos.

As Christians, we destabilize our faith if we place doctrinal emphasis upon one aspect of God as Father, Son, or Holy Spirit, and in doing so deny of the full nature of the Trinity. Ultimately, we see evidence of the principle of *panarchy* even in our limited understanding of the complex system of relationship of the Trinitarian God.

Calling the attention of the British Council of Churches, to this doctrinal weakness in the early 1980's, James B. Torrance, as chairman, helped lead to a new renaissance of Trinitarian doctrine among Christians. His older brother, Thomas F. Torrance, in an essay, "The Christ Who Loves Us," reminds us, saying, "…the Christ whom we love is fully one with God the Father. We are introduced to the word *homoousion*, which is the Greek for 'of the same being' Jesus and the Father are *homoosios, of one being with each other."* *Therefore, "God is not one thing in Christ and another in Himself." This has profound implications for us. Among them is the astonishing news that, "God loves us more than he loves himself!"[6]*

We seem continually prone to the weakness and dysfunction of developing bias for a single variable within a complex systems which cannot be simplified. Thus in the early Church of the second century, the teaching that the great Church Father, Augustine of Hippo, most dedicated himself to was *The Trinity.*[7] Augustine was fully aware the great Roman philosopher Cicero had also meditated on triads, notably on memory, mind/intellect, and will.[8]

It is tempting to confine the recognition that we human beings may be predisposed to ignoring the principle of *panarchy* to some detached system of logic or a philosophical arguments, but a more appropriate response would seem to require personal embodiment.

As Christian leaders, that task of embodiment must always begin with the experience of being embraced by the Father, be-graced by Jesus Christ, and empowered by the Holy Spirit. Here we receive a vast God-given source

6. Thomas F. Torrance, "The Christ Who Loves Us", in *A Passion For Christ: The Vision That Ignites Us*, edit. *Thomas F. Torrance, James B. Torrance, David W. Torrance (*Edinburgh: The Handsel Press, and PLC Publications, 1999), p.9.

7. Saint Augustine, *The Trinity,* trans. Edmund Hill O.P. (Brooklyn: New City Press, 1991).

8. *Ibid,* bk. xiv: 12

and incentive that will prepare us to serve in the complexity and difficulty of the real world like no others ever can. Yet such boldness is never possible, other than with the humility of Christ. Augustine clearly saw and exemplified this centrality of humility. As he shares in *The Confessions,* his earlier work, humility is never executed self-consciously, only in the consciousness of divine humility. Aggressiveness, zeal, double-mindedness, political tactics, enthusiasm, will never win the skepticism of colleagues; only humility is winsome and empowering.

Likewise, to recognize and respond to the single-variable optimization that triggers *panarchy* in the market-place must first begin with doing so in the home, for behavior is a continuum. Ted Ward, who had directed the Values Development Education Center, at Michigan State University, argued that business leaders engages their colleagues as they engage with their family. Family values can be taught to a child using a hand - five fingers: physical, mental, emotional, social, and moral, the palm symbolizing "the spiritual core". Values for the company begin with the values in the home. Likewise, we must work to reconcile the secular and the sacred. There are not two "kingdoms" as Martin Luther taught, in the separation of church and state, the secular and the religious, the academy and the church.[9] This sequesters the church into a form of institutional religion, and sets up the false opposition of choices that make "business sense" competing

9. T.F. Torrance, *Theology in Reconstruction* (Eugene, OR: Wipf & Stock, 1996).

against ones that make "moral sense". This seems to set a path toward crisis, not wisdom or truth.

All social sustainability requires transparency. Without it truth cannot prevail. Smoke and mirrors, whether in bureaucracy or in church governance, or in business leadership, paralyses ethical action and future well-being. Long-range planning, implementation of decisions, and all the advice sought after, can be a total waste of time without the exercise of transparency. We are plagued with the pandemic of a lack of transparency between each other today, and suffering the consequences of moral failure it often causes or allows. We need to change this reality in our governments, our churches and our companies. However, businesses have one great advantage over religious institutions on these matters - they can reinvent themselves rapidly. Whereas religious institutions can linger, while their credibility wanes, for a very long time!

Questions for Further Reflection

1. What moral duties does society expect of persons but not corporations with respect to the "commons"? What "commons" are you part of that may be at risk of overuse? How about your company, your church? (FGS p. 10)
2. In what areas of your life are you optimizing too much a single variable and thus risking a response of panarchy? What might you need to do to adopt a "systems

thinking" approach to those issues and find greater balance and become more aware of your own identity? (FGS p.10)

3. How does being a Christian allow us to let go of the need to try to gain mastery of all aspects of our world? How might you better respond to that freedom? (FGS p. 16-17)

4. In what ways has God stitched together unique parts of your own story to prepare you for what you face now?

1

Why Business Ethics?

Asking "why?" has great power, for it challenges the way we think, and how we behave.[1] For we should never assume others think the same way we do. For that reason, it may require great courage to raise such a simple, yet profound question in the board rooms and halls of our businesses. It can stir up a hornet's nest! Constantly asking ourselves "why?" can give us a very dynamic life, for we find nothing is ever "normal". It usually means we are emotionally asleep when things always appear "normal". Being truly yourself by asking "why?" can make you the stranger among your colleagues. Or it can be a lightning rod that disperses all the pent-up frustration between colleagues. For "why?" is not asked by bureaucrats. "Why?" belongs to the interpretation of reality that is intrinsically relational.[2]

Money is inert, and a-moral, and gold simply a mineral deposit in the earth, which is of course the very rea-

1. Amanda Lang, *The Power of Why* (Toronto: Harper Collins, 2012).
2. Simon Sinek, *Start with Why: How Great Leaders inspire Everyone to Take Action* (New York: Portfolio Penguin, 2009).

son we need business ethics. At the beginning of the 20th century, the German sociologist, Georg Simmel asked the question "why?" about the nature of money, and the nature of society; and indeed, about the nature of human culture. So he speaks of "exchange of goods" as a social interaction. The more relational it becomes, the richer the social interaction. A jeweler buys diamonds wholesale as a low form of interaction, but a lover buying a diamond ring has a far richer social interaction.

The source of value is not economic, it is social. Financial exchanges are simply elaborating the social category of exchange, whether institutionally or individually. How we value money then is a manifestation of sociability. With innumerable forms of social life, it can be "with-one-another," "for one another," "in-one-another," "against one-another," and "through one-another," in family, friendships, communities, and states, clubs and churches.[3]

The question "why business ethics?" begins by distinguishing ethics from morals. The moral agent is primarily individual, not social. Ethics is about individual choices and decisions, whereas morals are social. Immanuel Kant devised his theory of a moral universe, as opposed to a personal one. This theory ultimately collapsed with all abstractions of Romanticism, Socialism, Fascism and

---

3. Georg Simmel, *On Individuality and Social Forms,* edit. Donald N. Levine (Chicago: The University of Chicago Press, 1971), "On Sociability," p.127.

Communism in the twentieth century. Post-Modernism is now picking up the pieces in the ruins.

Likewise, business executives cannot blame the corporate culture they inhabit; they are judged as individuals in their responses to the status-quo. As we know day-to-day, "the buck stops here." Then we can expect immediate action. Hence, we see the folly of bureaucracy, and now also the new folly of the automation of business practice. The automation of production, yes, but the dominance of artificial intelligence, no! That will create even worse chaos than the collective ideologies of the past. A human world requires human accountability.

The Omnipotence of Money

Again we ask, "why business ethics?" It is because the blind monetization of the Market has great impacts on Religion, Politics, and Law, as well as on Ethics, which we have just discussed. In religious language, money is a "god-term" for the vast majority of the human race. Georg Simmel calls it, "the omnipotence of money." It is the all-determining reality of human existence. That is why Mammon is the prevailing god of this age.

As Christians, we should note how it takes center-stage in the life and ministry of Jesus. Ben Witherington, has shown how money takes center-stage in his public life.[4] His parables are replete over the issues

4. Ben Witherington, *Jesus and Money: a Guide for Times of Financial Crisis* (Grand Rapids, MI: Baker, 2010). P. 111.

of handling money, while his whole ministry was so profoundly related to money issues, as He cleansed the temple of its traffickers, and how He was eventually betrayed by the bribery given to Judas. Nothing should be more important for all Christians than the demonization of money. This is done on a daily basis by reading the Gospels, and meditating all the time how Jesus faced its demons on a daily basis. For we all have a 'porosity' of our souls and psyche, never free from the lure of money. Fear and money, these are two basic constituents of our emotional life, as it was in the life of the Jews.

Another writer, Gary Inrig, has shown the financial wisdom we can gain from the parables of Jesus.[5] There is the folly of accumulation of wealth in the parable of the rich fool (Lk.12:13-21). It leads to the downward spiral of greed, an insatiable beast. For living 'well' is far more than having 'more'. Again, the parable of the shrewd manager (Lk. 16:8-13) demonstrates the enormous power 'mammon' (i.e. both money and possessions) can have over us. It can have eternal consequences, for good or evil. We have to choose between God and money; we cannot serve both. The parable of the rich young ruler (Matt.19:16-26), defines how and what we define as 'rewards', from a temporal or from an eternal perspective? The parable of the workers in the vineyard (Matt. 20: 1-16) again tests the motivation of discipleship; why do we serve the Lord?

5. Gary Inrig, *Your Money Matters: Financial Wisdom from the Parables of Jesus* (Grand Rapids, MI: Discovery House Publishers, 2014).

Profoundly then, do our Lord's parables give us wisdom about handling money.

There is a lot to say also in how the apostle Paul faces the challenges of collecting and of using money. Verlyn D. Verbrugge & Keith R. Krell, explore this in their book, *Paul and Money.*[6] Paul's reluctance to accept monetary support in 1 Corinthians 9, 1 Thessalonians 2:1-9, and 2 Thessalonians 3:6-15, is further communicated in Colossians 1:24 and Galatians 6:17. He challenges issues of patronage, and of showing concern for the poor, as well as of challenging the rich about the treatment of the poor in the house churches. Paul generates a massive collection for the famine relief of the brethren in Palestine, with its complications of gathering and distributing. All of this focus upon money in the ministry and teaching of Paul, lead David Downs to say that we can distinguish the spurious letters attributed to Paul by the fact they make no mention of money matters.[7]

Another aspect of Pauline ethics, is his theme of friendship and finances. He devotes the whole of his epistle to the Philippians to this delicate subject, while it is clearly a major theme in his personal letter to Philemon over his run-away-slave. Money which is still a delicate matter between friends, was no less so for Paul and his

6. Verlyn D. Verbrugge & Keith R. Krell, *Paul & Money: a Biblical and Theological Analysis of the Apostle's Teachings and Practices* (Grand Rapids, MI: Zondervan, 2015).

7. David Downs, "Paul's Collection and the Book of Acts Revisited." *New Testament Studies*. Volume 52(1) (Cambridge: Cambridge University Press, 2006), p. 50.

communities. So, in his *peroration* of Philippians 4:4-20, he recapitulates all he has already communicated, to create *pathos,* that is the deepest emotions, such as love, joy, peace, which come from the presence of the Lord in our lives. For the example of Christ in our lives, is the unique source of Christian ethics, whether it is about friendship, money, or anything else. Now Christians have to work it all out (Phil. 4:1-19). This is all so beautifully commented upon by Ben Witherington, *Friendship and Finances in Philippi.*[8]

Applying these Biblical principles is then a serious challenge for all Christians. This challenge is well spelled out in a recent series of essays, edited by Jurgen von Hagen and Michael Welker, *Money As God?* [9] As it concludes, it asks us to reflect on three propositions:

1. Monetization causes far-reaching changes in a society.
2. Money, by making everything comparable, contributes to the dissolution of valuable social relationships.
3. Money is dangerous, because it distracts human trust from God to trust in dead material things.

8. Ben Witherington, *Friendship and Finances in Philippi* (Valley Forge, PA: Trinity Press International, 1994), pp. 110-133.

9. Jurgen von Hagan and Michael Welker, *Money as God: The Monetization of the Market and its Impact on Religion, Politics, Law, and Ethics* (Cambridge: Cambridge University Press, 2014).

Mammon as God in Our Society

Another important author is our Regent colleague Craig Gay, who has written several important books, beginning with his basic sociological thesis that money is the god of this society.[10]

Monetization, in turn, gives shape to human desire. We all are aware we live in a consumer society and culture. But it cannot be any single definition of a consumer culture, since it is all bound up with our history, past and present. Even being a 'consumer' may mean being frugal or profligate, poor or rich. The salesman knows he can sell 'dreams' or he can sell tangible objects. As a Chrysler flyer states: "DRIVE= LOVE". If you can buy the car to drive, can you also buy love? The blurring of the lines between fact and fiction are always there, as we all know in our credit culture. As the Thompson Red Book, the pioneer in the new advertising world put it a century ago: "Advertising aims to teach people that they have wants, which they did not recognize before, and where such wants can be best supplied."

This is precisely why business ethics should be about teaching people to desire better things, and not about the proliferation of unhealthy or dangerous desires, whether

---

10. Craig M. Gay, *The Way of the (Modern) World, or Why it's Tempting to Live as if God Doesn't Exist* (Grand Rapids, MI: Wm. B. Eerdmans, 1998).

it is about what we eat, or the possession of dangerous weapons, to quiet our fears.

The Psalms are replete with the voices of the poor, as are the homilies on the Psalms which the great Father of the Church, Augustine preached weekly over eighteen years. Uniquely, too, he explores the nature of human desire. His basic argument is that since God created us, our primary desire is for Him alone. But when this gets diverted, we are left unsatisfied by lesser objects of desire. This disquietude penetrates to the roots of our being, leading him to speak of the "restless heart," for which there is no quietude except God alone. It becomes "an insatiable demand for desire," which is incurable apart from God.

But it does explain market forces today, where money is society's god, explaining consumer restlessness. This clarifies the Christian perspective the pursuit of business ethics, as matching desire with object, in faithfulness and commitment.[11]

Questions for Further Reflection

1. How do you experience the balance of *ipse* and *idem* in your life, and how to you observe it in others? What 3 things might you do to pursue deeper knowledge and balance of these two formational aspects of your identity? (FGS p. 17-18)

2. "A human world requires human accountability." Who helps you to be creative and steadfast in pursu-

11. *Ibid,* p. 439.

ing ethical behavior? What people or groups are you accountable to?

3. Resisting mammon as god must be a daily exercise or else we should be likely to conform to the patterns of society. What habits or exercises do you have that help resist mammon, and instead confess Jesus as Lord?

2

The Failure of Success

The rich and the famous are those who most ironically experience "the failure of success". For money and fame will never substitute for a broken marriage and troubled children. What is true of the family is likewise true of the culture, as Charles Taylor has critiqued in his CBC Massey lectures, "The Malaise of Modernity". He begins by describing three worries: the rise of individualism; the primacy of instrumental reason; the rise of soft despotism, where voluntarism fades with the domination of bureaucracy. The failure to delegate in business, can readily generate all three of these "worries". Of course, one leader can do things much more efficiently than a rival. But a culture of individualism can create havoc in a co-operative venture which a business always is.

The failure to create a co-operative governance balanced by individual responsibility, can generate what Taylor calls the failure of authenticity, when all is focused on the individual's sincerity, authenticity, private motives and moralism. This can be very subtle, hence Taylor's central chapters require deep reflection. Moral fragmentation is a consequence within the company. This generates powerlessness, that we can do nothing to remedy the morale and consequences of fragmentation. In political terms, this implies that federalism and monarchy are a wiser form of governance than the greater forms of centralization in other countries of the world.

The Failure of Reductionism

For the Christian, the great mandate of Deuteronomy 6 is the foundation:

> Hear O Israel: The Lord our God, the Lord is one. Love the Lord your God with all your heart and with all your soul and with all your strength. These commandments that I give you today are to be on your hearts. Impress them on your children. Talk about them when you sit at home and when you walk along the road, when you lie down and when you get up. Tie them as symbols on your hands and bind them on your foreheads. Write them on the doorframes of your houses and on your gates." (Deut. 6: 3-9)

It means there should be no difference between the morals of office and home, company and family. It implies such moral sustainability is passed on from generation to generation.

As a young professor at Oxford and colleague of C.S. Lewis later in his life, I once asked him what all his writings were centered upon, and if perhaps there was a summary to the diverse genres he so skillfully exercised and expressed. His response was, "it is simply the refutation of reductionism." In the University of Oxford, he was fighting against philosophy being reduced to logical positivism, and against science becoming scientism, and against literary criticism becoming a mere technique of criticism. Meanwhile, he himself lived a double life, between his home life tyrannized by Mrs. Moore, and his lively, debating life with his fellow dons at High Table. Yet he had deep prescience of the coming Tech revolution as an omni-present technical culture, which now is challenging us all so deeply. His educational lectures describe "Men without Chests", de-humanized by reductionism. While his science fiction novel, *That Hideous Strength*, describes the human distortions that occur with scientism, when *homo sapiens* inevitably turns first into mere *homo sciens*, and then into mere *nature*.

It is what the poet T.S. Eliot anticipated in 1924, with his poem, "The Waste Land."

> Where is the wisdom, we have lost in knowledge?
> Where is the knowledge we have lost in information?
> The cycle of twenty centuries
> Take us further from God
> And nearer to the dust.

The Failure of Misguided Desire

We could say, "the failure of success," follows upon pinning our hopes on the wrong desires. This is illustrated globally by the environmental crisis, where human beings are squandering the Earth's resources in consumerism. Geological cycles of mineral renewal, and agricultural cycles of food resources, are unsustainable for the infinite desires of human beings. This is simply illustrated in *For Goodness' Sake* as, "the tragedy of the commons." In the medieval English village, there was a shared common land, sustainable as long as the villagers each considered the interests of the others, as well as the sustainability of the land.

The preservation of the common land, in restraints placed on human desire, however did not begin with the village lands of Medieval England. It began in remote pre-history, still exhibited among some Amazonian tribes, still attached deeply to their lands. In the UNESCO preserve of one tribe of the Venezuelan Amazon, their bodies and faces are inscribed with cosmic symbols that depict the superior forces that determine their behavior as being in harmony within the rhythm of Nature. They do not articulate that they are created in the *Imago Dei,* but all their desires and behavior clearly illustrate this as being embodied on their faces. As a result, such primitive tribes still maintain far greater sustainability with simple desires and needs, in contrast to our highly complex desires and uninhibited greed.

Survival and sustainability are human twins. There is no survival without sustainability, as there is no human life without morals. Again, citing primitive man, there is the Minoan myth in the island of Crete, of the golden thread of Ariadne. The goddess spun it, to save the life of Theseus in the underground labyrinth. Following the thread, he was able to navigate the labyrinth, reaching the outside world once more in well-being.[1] "Sustainability" is our Ariadne's golden thread, the traceable theme throughout this book, for all business practice depends upon it.

Questions for Further Reflection

1. How might we begin to put rationalism in its more proper place as a complement to other avenues by which we gain wisdom in our businesses, churches and our own lives? (FGS p. 15)
2. What can you do to continue to more fully rediscover your *selfless gene*? (FGS p. 21)
3. As our desire for mammon (money) is a misguided desire that will leave us feeling empty when fulfilled, what other empty or misguided desires are common in our society? What contributes to making them alluring to you?

1. J.D. Hughes, edit. "Pan: Environmental Crisis in Classical Polytheism" in *Religion and Environmental Crisis* (Athens, GA: University of Georgia Press, 1986).

3

For Goodness' Sake: Business for Telos 1

The reminder that we are "relational beings" is in many ways, the thrust of this book. Because all human beings are made in the *imago dei,* so we are more afraid of each other, than with the external world. Fear is our basic emotion and dominates all other human emotions. Fear is much more intrinsic than extrinsic. As in the famous novel of the Nobel prize-winner, William Golding, has the school-boys confess, in *Lord of the Flies,* "I'm afraid of us." Or as Jean Paul-Sartre expressed, "Hell is other people." Since business is so intrinsically relational, to escape from fear and to be freed from our own neurotic behaviors may just be the primary cause of any "good business" that should result.

What Then Is Goodness?

The original meaning of the word "good" or "goodness" has a basic theme of bringing together, of uniting. It implies a whole range of beneficial effects for others, such as: well-behaved, honest, worthy of respect, virtuous, pure, commendable, as well as useful, suited to the purpose, skillful and competent, thorough, valid, right, just, and desirable. Goodness then, like love, casts out all fear. With its associated virtues, they all reflect what a good business relates and reflects with its customers, employees, and colleagues, as well as its external relations with the world.

It is what the Oxford philosopher Iris Murdoch called in a series of lectures later developed into the book, *The Sovereignty of Good Over Other Concepts*. She spelled out some of the characteristics of this concept. Good, she proposed, should be realistic, not idealistic, although it can be commended as an ideal.[1] Yet it exists in a world where human beings are naturally selfish, as self-contained and without social purpose.

Plato hints (in *Phaedrus,* 250) that "unselfing" is possible, when we can admire beauty, either in painting, works of art, or indeed in music. These arts create a quality of excellence that provides an inspiring environment, for their purpose is not consoling one's self, but giving beneficially to others. As Iris Murdoch says: "the enjoyment of art is a training in the love of virtue."[2] For again, following Plato, she held that beauty could be a good starting point of the good life. Both in the arts and in intellectual disciplines, we discover value in the ability to forget ourselves and to be realistic, and to perceive justly. They enable us accept the authority of truth and reality. We receive courage for our convictions, and clarity of purpose for our ac-

1. Iris Murdoch, *The Sovereignty of Good Over Other Concepts* (Cambridge: Cambridge University Press, 1967).
2. *Ibid*, p. 13

tions. These would seem to be essential developments in the cultivation of the practice of "good business."

In a world that is aimless, chancy, and vast, we need a magnetic compass for our navigation, a center for our motives, which is why we latch on to values like goodness and love, seeing both having a reciprocal mutuality. What is good is loveable, what is loveable is good. But without Christ, neither is a definable reality. As Iris Murdoch sadly states: "I think Good and Love should not be identified, and not only because human love is usually self-assertive... Good is the magnetic center towards which love naturally moves. False love moves to false good."[3] For her, a "god" was false love, as she saw the inconsistent behavior of Christians around her. Her novels deeply penetrate the human psyche, but nowhere does she see divine love expressed, unlike her colleague C.S. Lewis. She died in the lost wilderness of dementia, without awareness of the gift of God as our Eternal Memory.

Glenn Tinder, a political scientist, has raised the question, "can we be good without God?"[4] Such values as good and love need metaphysical foundations. Then love for Christians is the highest standard of human relationships, and it is also unique, utterly different from all kinds of love. For God is love, which is why the early Church used the term *agape*, having only reference to Christian

3. *Ibid,* p. 35
4. Glenn Tinder, *Can We Be Good Without God? On the Political Meaning of Christianity* (Regent College Reprints: Vancouver, 1993).

love.[5] *Agape* therefore is transcendent over "the good," whereas in contrast, Iris Murdoch could only conceive of goodness and love in a bi-lateral relationship.

The capability to bring to life these concepts of "love" and "the good" ultimately rests in a union with God through relationship.

This can lead to an exalted view of the individual, especially in situations where power is wielded, such as politics and business. This of course means that "care" must be exercised in the wielding of power, which inevitably requires more demanding standards for those who hold such power and influence.

The Transcendence of Love Over Good

The absolute good for the Christian is that God is our creator. And not only is He our creator, but, as we are reminded in the words of Genesis, He saw all He had created as "good" and humans as "very good." More personally, God is also my Redeemer, causing the ongoing transformation of a sinner destined for the consequences of sin into one forgiven and destined for eternal glory. Our eternal joy depends upon God. Furthermore, all our relations with other human beings now become value-responses like no

5. *Ibid,* p. 5

other value responses.[6] They become unique in Him.

Paradoxically, "doing good" involves that we should continue at the task, as William Langland the Medieval Reformer, expounded in his allegory of the pilgrim, moving from "doing-good," to "doing better," to "doing best."[7] This involves the will, the willingness to exceed. But a second dimension of this lies in the totality of response, now involving the whole person. This now involves the heart, as a value of self-donation, indeed of the motivation of *charis* love. Happiness is another dimension, as it produces joy to share such goodness and love.

In his remarkable book, von Hildebrand speaks of, "the incomparable transcendence of moral-value response", primarily of the will to morally relevant goods.[8] But the involvement of the heart is always motivating more, as we have seen. It implies too, the conquest of evils such as concupiscence and pride, by now having delight in doing good. As St. Augustine expressed it: "It is not enough for us to be moved by the will, we must also be moved by delight."[9] There flows then from the transcendence of love, the yearning for unity with one's colleagues, the longing for reciprocity of concern, and all the mani-

6. Dietrich von Hildebrand, *The Nature of Love,* trans. John F. Crosby with John Henry Crosby (South Bend, Indiana: St. Augustine's Press, 2009), pp. 119-121.

7. Nevill Coghill, *Visions from Piers Plowman, A New Rendering of Langland's Original* (New York: Oxford University Press, 1970).

8. von Hildebrand, *op. cit.*, p.85

9. St. Augustine, *Tractate 26 on the Gospel of St. John.*

festations of what *caritas* is described to be, by the Apostle Paul in I Corinthians 13.

Questions for Further Reflection

1. We sometimes see negative aspects of the "4th voice" (FGS p. 26) – or what we might call "negative populism"– that can sometimes (even often) overwhelm the more positive aspects of the "4th voice" – or what we might call "positive populism". How are Christians serving as both participants and counter-note to these patterns? How might we?

2. In what areas of your life is it especially tempting for you to love or appreciate the good more than the *source* of the good? (i.e. to "love the gift more than the giver?")

4

Purpose for Business: Byproducts of Unrest

Anything that has a "purpose" necessarily has an objective in view. From the latin *propositum*, it reflects a design, or an intention; it has an aim. For the ancient Egyptians, the purpose of art was to arouse admiration. Later for the Greeks, *telos* originally was exercised in pursuit of honor through action. Purpose also gives cohesion. So the Greek *telos* being primarily the pursuit of *arête* or excellence expressed a heroic culture. Ulysses exemplifies the exploring instinct in man, all to gain honor from and within the city state, just as the Olympian games gained physical prowess.

One of my senior colleagues could not understand why I should ever volunteer to leave Oxford, for a whole new vocation. So he kindly gave me a book, *The Ulysses Factor,* to explain it all![1]

Purpose has always generated arousal to make changes from the *status quo.* The Greek philosopher Pericles applied purpose to the making of money, saying, "As for poverty, no one need be ashamed to admit it; the real shame is not taking the practical measures to escape

1. J.R.L. Anderson, *The Ulysses Factor: The Exploring Instinct in Man* (London: Houghton & Stoughton, 1970).

from it."[2] Not surprisingly, exploring and making money still dominate the landscape.

However, today, more and more sustainable business organizations are recognizing that what will sustain them has to be serving others. *For Goodness' Sake* is clearly defining this ethic of being a "self-for-the-other". Money does not in itself motivate our best intentions nor morals. But service does: it brings out the best in people, enables creative action, and empowers people to do great, creative things. For it also connects people together, which individualism can never accomplish. This is where real purpose is found.

Choices of Purpose

When it comes to purpose, we must all understand we have a choice to make. What we purpose differs greatly, whether it is Greek in its heroism, Stoic in its Latin morality, or selfless in its Christian foundations. The pursuit of Greek 'honor' and Stoic moralism were really all for self-glory, as the pursuit of money still is!

Henry Ford might have proclaimed he was building the people's car "to democratize the automobile", but ends and means were curiously reversed, for the outputs were

2. Quoted in C.M. Bowra, *The Greek Experience (London: Weidenfeld and Nicolson, 1959)*, p.22.

the means for his ultimate end, exercising *his* own will to improve *his* world.

The philosopher Friedrich Nietzsche was appalled by democracy, which he thought mediocre: for he still lived with Napoleonic dreams. Instead, he embraced the heroic model, which required military courage, pride, and firmness, found only in a few great leaders. But such romanticizing of egos was implicated in the build up of Hitler and his followers, and in other tragedies of the twentieth century. Nietzsche proposed we should shun Christianity and compassion, and rather embrace "great men" (*ubermensch*) like Napoleon. For Christianity, he believed, sought to tempt us to think that there was, "no fundamental difference in value between the elite and the masses… ideas that have resulted in a dwarfed, almost ludicrous species…something sickly, mediocre, the European of the present day."[3]

And yet today, in another repudiation of Nietzschean ideals, we are witnessing the crash of huge corporations that seem to reflect his "heroic model", like Siemens in Brazil, or Volkswagen in Germany, both of which originated in the 1930's and benefited from the use of slave labor under the Nazi regime. Samsung shows the same signs of Nietzschean behavior in the disdain its leaders

3. Nikos Mourkogiannis, *PURPOSE: the Starting Point of Great Companies* (New York: St.Martin's Press, 2006) p. 36.

have shown for its stock-holders and clients in defrauding them in order to make more money for themselves.

Categories of Moral Purpose

Very helpfully, Nikos Mourkogiannis distinguishes categories of moral purpose in the following table[4]:

Moral	Type of Morality	Moral Basis for Action	Philosopher	Company
Discovery	"The New"	Free choice	Kierkegaard	IBM
Excellence	"The Good"	Fulfilment	Aristotle	Apple
Altruism	"The Helpful"	Happiness	Hume	Wal-Mart
Heroism	"The Effective"	Achievement	Nietzsche	Ford Motor Co.

Telos then, has its historical roots in diverse moralities, chosen by differing businesses in different contexts. For there is no "purpose" in the abstract. It always needs a historical context. Some companies arose in the need for patriotism, as Hyundai sought to provide in the re-unification of Korea. While Toyota sought to re-build the shattered Japanese economy after World War II. And today, President Trump is now reviving the concept of patriotic business to promote his protectionist agenda.

Universalism is another purpose. It is the purpose behind the railways, the postal services, and the nation-

4. *Ibid,* p.37.

al health industries. The philosophers, Hume and Kant sought universal moralism, in the roles played by emotion and reason respectively, to bring unity of purpose.

Legalism, another purpose, has generated after the rise of the Enlightenment, such a unifying national identities as Scotland. For in the Scottish Enlightenment, the country adopted Roman Dutch law, in distinction from English common law. To this day, its corporations have a strong fiduciary sense of trust. Its business houses are not just 'institutions', merely created for whatever purpose one desires, but they act as 'institutes', having a strong sense of fiduciary trusteeship.[5] It explains why the legal profession has sustained a prominent social and political role in Scotland, unlike that of the rest of the United Kingdom.

But legality can be abused as legalism, as we see with so many bureaucratic institutions. Some of our worst examples are actually in our own churches. Then *telos* simply evaporates. Alas, Christians can be some of the worst kind of bureaucrats, as our church meetings regularly display! Then we need to closely examine how Jesus himself was provoked to anger by the Temple authorities, who were archetypes of religious bureaucracy.

As Vibeke Norgaard Martin has observed, "lawyers must be honest, but they don't have to be truthful," and "lawyers are contextualists," meaning that truth and transparency are not needed, only certain facts in relationship to other things. They have also noted that, "the law creates

5. Both terms 'institution' and 'institute' are clearly distinguished in the first edition of the Encyclopedia Britannica of 1764.

fictional characters," and, "the integrity of the legal system is more important to the court than the truth of one's case."[6]

Calling and the Christian Work Ethic

"Purpose" for Christians should have a contrastive work ethic. Max Weber traced this back to the Reformation in his classic, *The Protestant Ethic and the Spirit of Capitalism.* It was composed as two long essays (in 1904-5), then as a book. It hailed a new spirit, that was based on freedom, not slavery, which exercised rational intelligence, in continuous enterprise, and within an 'open' society. It emancipated the moral agent from the historical legacy of Rome, to enter a new world, wholly different from the past. But while it embraced Martin Luther's pragmatism, it did not understand the unitary nature of Luther's theology.

For while Luther saw the "right hand of God" in relational spiritual governance of families and communities, he spoke of "the left hand of God" governing work occupations and the business economy. He saw all human work as worship of God, taking place in every calling. Indeed, Luther exhorts us to recognize work as the holiest of callings, saying: "hear what your work is: it is the holiest thing, by which God is made glad and through which he will give and grant you his blessing." This exaltation of work should be applied to all tools… So see that "a devout

6. Vibeke Norgaard Martin with Matthew Frederick, *101 Things I Learned in Law School* (New York: Grand Central Publishing, 2013).

Christian farmer write on his wagon and plow, a shoe-maker on his leather and awl, a smith and a carpenter on their wood and iron this verse: 'Rejoice, for it is well with you!'[7]

Likewise, Luther's understanding of work as one's *vocation* or calling, was not as a job in which one was engaged to support oneself, nor as a profession, but as 'a calling', indeed a way of life.[8] John Calvin built on Luther's theology, preaching that worldly success was evidence of divine favor, of being one of the elect, predestined for eternal life. Not surprisingly, this gave a great impetus to Christian business men entering the Industrial Revolution in the nineteenth century, with new idealism for doing business. The Quaker Joseph Rowntree, used his chocolate business to also promote charity, in the adverse environment of the abusive greed that characterized the Industrial Revolution. Such Christian business men shone like beacons of philanthropy and Christian charity.

But again this Reformed theology has degenerated once more in our day, with the populist evangelists of "prosperity gospel", to hallow greed and corrupt morals of tax evasion in their so-called 'churches'. Ironically, some Islamic' led businesses, and the Parsee ethics of The Tata

7. Cited by Hans-Martin Barth, *The Theology of Martin Luther* (Minneapolis: Fortress Press, 2009), p.326.

8. *Ibid,* pp. 19-20.

group in India, have a far more religious ethical presence in their factories.

The real inheritance of the Protestant work ethic in America to-day, is represented by companies like ServiceMaster, whose motto is "To honor God in all we do".[9]

Questions for Further Reflection

1. How do you find joy and fulfillment in serving others? Whom do you feel most called to serve? How about your company? Your church?
2. Where would you place those answers on the "categories of moral purpose" chart above? How does that help you better consider the "change for the better" you might wish to see in those places?
3. What journey do you think the people in your organization might need to go on to more fully answer the above question and begin the path toward positive change?

9. Nikos Mourkogiannis, *op.cit.*, p. 39.

5

For Goodness' Sake: Business for Telos 2

The reversal of what businesses do, from profit as purpose, to profit that serves purpose, is a huge sea-change. We may, following Charles Taylor call it *metanoia*, as a profound cultural change. This is quite different from reform, and indeed all the other 're' words we use, that suggest change like: re-form, re-furbish, re-gain, re-new, re-invigorate, etc. Business and church life do these things all the time, just as we make 'new resolutions', every new Year. But *metanoia* is a completely new thing.

Rather the Greek *metamorphosis* is used by Homer as a miraculous transformation into a new shape, such as a stone might suddenly become a snake - indeed as Moses' rod became a serpent - so *metanoia* refers to a paradigm shift of mind, from the previous *habitus* or mind-set.

But *metanoia,* in its radicalism, cannot refer simply to cultural change, for it is intimately personal. Charles Taylor cites the example of Dante, who was a worldly aristocrat of Florence, then changed into a beggar wandering for the next phase of his life as a fugitive, fleeing to survive. Or it is like Dostoyevsky, a dissolute youthful rebel of the Czar, now standing blind-fold before the firing squad who will dispatch him and his comrades within five minutes into eternity; suddenly a Czar messenger brings a clemency to the group. Like, Dante, the experience of *metanoia* then wholly transformed the life of Dostoyevsky.

Business leaders do not usually experience such dramatic changes. Unless, perhaps they are miraculously saved from a heart surgery or a deadly cancer. Or if their business goes bankrupt and wonderfully, they recover in a new business enterprise. Then the recovery is much more than innovation, or a renewal of business as usual. It is a monumental and pivotal change.

This is what *For Goodness' Sake* calls "telosity" which is the result of metanoia that causes people in the company to change their behavior, and ultimately shifts the whole climate of the organization, its employees and customers, and even its philosophy and purpose, so that it moves toward becoming a "purposeful enterprise".

We are living in an era of rapid changes. We now have philosophical debates between economists and psychologists, to introduce the new discipline of behavioral economics, since the 1970's. This new brand of economists now desires to improve the explanatory and predictive power of economics, by using the theoretical and methodological resources of psychology. This raises expectations of having more realistic notions of human emotions incorporated into the business world.[1] But no sooner is

---

1. Stefan Heidl, *Philosophical Problems of Behavioural Economics* (London: Routledge, 2016).

this launched, than new perspectives begin to query these new attitudes!

Having a Changed Identity

Becoming "born again" seemed a cultural fad the press took up, when Chuck Colson spent time in prison for the Watergate cover-up.[2] Personally, he did experience *metanoia* when his aggressive political life lay shattered in ruins, and his *hubris* had seemingly destroyed his future. But Nixon underwent profound change too, sharing with Colson about his saintly Quaker Grandmother, who taught him: "Richard, …the purpose of prayer is to listen to God, not to talk to God. The purpose of prayer is not to tell God what thee wants, but to find out from God what He wants from thee."[3] Nixon had forgotten this, but he recovered the message. This is *metanoia* for every Christian, either when we accept the message for the first time, or we recover the message!

I met Chuck Colson shortly after he came out of prison, spending the next six months meeting with him twice weekly, to introduce him to the study of the Scriptures. Meanwhile, he was changing his intentions dramatically, working to create Prison Fellowship, first as a national, then as an international organization. Indeed, meeting

2. Charles W. Colson, *Born Again* (Old Tappan, New Jersey: Chosen Books, 1976).
3. *Ibid, p. 184.*

Colson and observing his transformation was one of the more remarkable things I have experienced in my life.

But I myself experienced inwardly at a later period, a gentler, slower change of my own identity. This began during the 1950's, when I began quietly to reject having a professional identity. It began at the end of the war, when I was a pioneer regional planner, and developed a strong reaction to Christians ever having a *professional identity.*

Having a functional identity grew strongly with the new professions created by the new universities after the war. Then I began to see that the clergy themselves, in insisting or being insisted upon by their congregants, to be called "Pastor X" or "Reverend Y" and carrying the same pseudo-identity. It has been the hardest change to try to initiate in my whole life. As Christians, we must not seek to have a functional identity; but rather to have a relational one as intrinsic to who we are, "in Christ."

Of course, such a Christian perspective is not new. It began when the world-view of Saul of Tarsus was shattered as a zealous reformer of Judaism, "a Pharisee of the Pharisees", when on the Damascus road, he saw Christ in His glory. This was the apostle Paul's *metanoia.* Mystical experiences still continue to transform people's lives today, whether of Moslems becoming Christians, or of Christians becoming more Christian.

But it was the Apostle Paul's insistence in disclosing 166 times in his epistles, of the Christian identity now being "in Christ", that gave rise to the prominence of Christianity in the Roman world. It all began very simply, as one personal experience, that then continued to grow in importance for the rest of the Apostle's life and ministry.

As *For Goodness' Sake* puts it, "others have gone before", so it is a mark of sobriety that we are foolish or proud to be too self-conscious of being involved in the adventure of *metanoia*. Having a purpose-for-others is as old as Neanderthal Man, when we discover the bone evidence of numerous burial chambers which were carefully prepared, and that their hunters had suffered bone injuries early in their lives. They could never have survived, as it seems they did, if the principle of "the self-for-the-other" had not been daily practiced. This was happening in the glacial age, 60,000 years ago! The "selfless gene" may not be much in evidence today, but one of the two origins of the evolution of man had it aplenty; the exception was *Homo sapiens.*[4]

Creative Imagination

Innovation, of course, does come from creative imagination. A modern philosopher, Paul Ricoeur considers this the most formidable of all studies, the human imagination. Intuition, he sees, as a reciprocity between two poles, the voluntary "I will" and the diversity of involuntary and intractable incapacities. The outcome is "I can" as a navi-

---

4. Elaborated in a forthcoming book by Theodore George and James M. Houston, *Freedom from Fear to Love.*

gation between the two poles.[5]

But creativity is enhanced by frustration, or by greater barriers that David Hurst calls "the back loop of renewal". A solid company is doing well, when suddenly some raider(s) steps in and bids to buy out the company. In the confusion of the administrators, it needs the clear judgment of the creative leadership of the leaders to make new choices, fateful as they may seem, to climb a new mountain of creative possibilities, unforeseen before the crisis. Then with trust in the new leadership the innovators take the company into a wholly new territory.

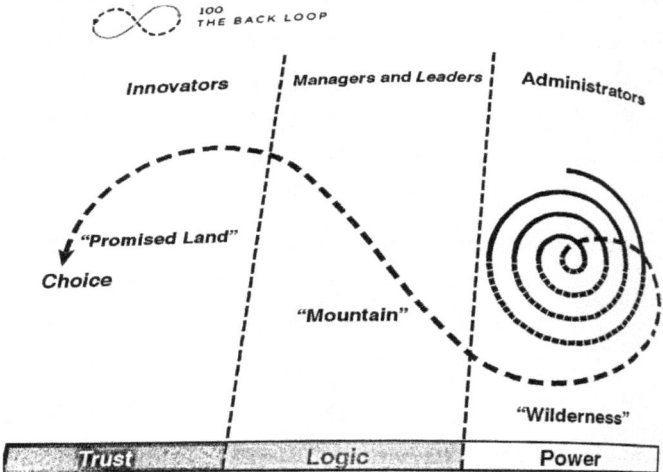

5. Henry Isaac Venema, *Identifying Selfhood: Imagination, Narrative, and Hermeneutics in the Thought of Paul Ricoeur* (Albany, NY: State University of New York Press, 2000), pp. 39-41.

As a Christian business consultant, David Hurst premises his back-loop theory upon the Biblical story of the Israelites, where the wandering in the wilderness is all about power struggles.[6] It is what happens when a business or a church community is entrapped in the bureaucratic governance of the administrators. Then a company will be going from banks to other lenders, to get out of the encircling maze. It is "a wandering in the wilderness." Systemic issues need to be dealt with and are not. Many large corporations have faced this "wilderness experience" in the last decades of the past century. Westinghouse, General Motors, even I.B.M. have had to re-invent themselves. Or, they may struggle to do so and fail to remain innovative. Many drug companies are finding themselves in this situation today, and in response they buy more and more smaller companies that have new drugs for the market, but once more systemic issues are not faced.

For Christians, all this process of *metanoia* can be summarized in the story of the Israelites under the leadership of Moses. We may think of it as a business having to move into three dramatic environments:

1. The Wandering in the Wilderness, represents the muddle, the stagnation, the crisis the company or the church is in, by staying with traditional practices, bureaucracy, and other expressions of traditional slow-

6. David Hurst, *The New Ecology of Leadership: Business Mastery in a Chaotic World* (New York: Columbia University Press, 2012).

down.

2. The vision from Mount Sinai, reflects the new leadership seeking to make radical change(s) as *metanoia.*
3. The entry into the Promised Land. This is when institutional change has deeply penetrated into the lives of all its community and institutional life.

Then we can describe the narrative of change as beginning with the visionary leader, as having seven stages for Moses, and all his successive leaders. For once on the mountain, as Moses had to climb, there is then the far more arduous task of creating a shared vision, that unites the whole community. Moses did this in giving the Israelites the ten commandments, which we shall interpret as the virtues of such transformative leadership. But the leader has first of all to exhibit and to embody personally these changes before he/she has credibility.

How Does the Leader Personally Change?

We will suggest there are seven changes required.

1. The will to make the change.
2. The strong purpose to climb the mountain.
3. Gaining the clarity of vision during 'the mountain climb', to gain a much broader perspective.
4. The personal changes occurring in the leader as 'the climber', in a self-transcendence that self-interest can

never have.

5. Seeking to generate the new shared vision, and to unite the community/work-force in the new tasks ahead.

6. Sustaining the new community spirit. For this the leader(s) cannot rely on personal rhetoric or on force of personality, for they have to integrate the group not by dominating it, but by expressing their shared feelings and convictions.

7. Like a 'spiritual mid-wife' the leader(s) delivers or brings to birth, the intuitive convictions of the group, stimulating what is the best in other people by being selfless. Such selfless leadership is always relative, as Moses himself became a failed leader, unable personally 'to enter the Land'.

What then is "the Promised Land"? It is not a territory but the ethical changes which transform the people of God to become His people, and then continue to live the rest of their lives by His promises alone. Then 'Trust' as trust in God becomes the true Sabbath rest. As the Psalmist expressed it: "In You, Lord my God, I put my trust". (Ps. 25:1) There the Psalmist has Sabbath rest. How little does Zionism understand that "the Promised Land" is still not a territory, but a condition of soul before God!

Yet businesses can be sustained in their "Promised Land", when the same principles are applied: selfless leadership, clear thinking, the freedom of delegation, deep loyalties to the whole community, expressive commitments, metaphorical and symbolic actions, and ongoing selfless leadership of the titular leaders. All of these contribute to create an environment of relational trust.

Questions for Further Reflection

1. In remembering that "others have always gone before" (FGS p. 46) – who do you look up to or count as an inspiration for pursuing the kinds of company or organization you hope to be a part of or living the kind of life you hope to live? Consider reading a biography or two of the leaders who inspire you.
2. In what areas of your life have you experienced *metanoia* and what changed as a result? (FGS p. 81) How has your identity been shaped by those experiences and resulting changes?
3. What "wilderness wanderings" are you engaging in right now that the Lord might be providing a way out of through the interest and influence of people you look up to as leaders in your life? How might you be doing the same for others?

6

How to Bring a Purposeful Enterprise to Life

For Goodness Sake describes three "transformational levers": choice (strategy), aspiration (culture), and embodiment (leadership).

Thoughts on "Choice"

The freedom to choose begins with one's self. You can choose to live a morally and spiritually paralyzed life or an active life. Paradoxically, many young people physically paralyzed by polio or sporting accidents live a far more purposed life than many of us who are bodily fit. Handicaps are no excuse! There are always remedies available, now, more than ever. So then, we create our own culture and environment around us, that reinforce who we are. Then we become our own prisoners of the self, within the self. When Paul and Silas were in the prison, they chose not to be prisoners of fear. When miraculously with the earthquake, they could have fled, they chose not to escape, then finding their prison guard more afraid of his own prisoners than they were of him. Actually, their fearlessness saved his life, when he was ready to commit suicide out of fear. The end of the story is that the jailor's whole household experienced *metanoia*! (Acts 16:16-34). As far as Peter was concerned, he had already experienced freedom from prison, when he had been previously imprisoned in Jerusalem, by Herod (Acts 12:1-18).

From this we learn that personal *metanoia* inspires and strengthens others to make choices too, whether inside or outside the business! If the choices we have to make are costly, they speak most strongly to others aware of their personal costliness. For *metanoia* never comes with easy choices; they are always hard decisions. Likewise, the bigger the organization, the harder is the inertia one has to overcome and change heroically. It is a fight of David and Goliath.

Again, the older and more traditional the company, the harder are the choices the leader and his executives may have to take, to bring about *metanoia*. The remarkable story of James E. Burke, C.E.O. of Johnson & Johnson the pharmaceutical giant is well known. On Wednesday morning, Sept. 29, 1982, a twelve-year girl, Mary Kellerman awoke with a sore throat and runny nose; by 7 am. She was dead! A capsule of Extra-Strength Tylenol had been administered to her, but a criminal had laced it with cyanide. Six other people died in Chicago, in what the police began to see was an act of urban terrorism. The C.E.O. was James E. Burke.[1]

The first action Burke took was to give all available information to the press. His transparency preserved the public trust in the company. He was never evasive in all questions, but faced them all, openly and truthfully. Public safety was at risk, therefore public knowledge must be given.

The second action Burke took was to re-communicate the "Credo" of the company. During the 1940's the legendary C.E.O. General Robert Wood Johnson II, had issued the Credo as the company's core values. It hung like the ten commandments in the offices of all executives, on some 150-200 office walls. It proclaimed: "Our first responsibility is to the doctors, nurses, and patients, to mothers and fathers and all others who use our products and services."[2] This told Burke and his colleagues, regardless of any external pressures from the Federal Bureau of Investigation, and from the Food and Drug Administration to recall all capsules, the company should act in the best interest of the people who used the product. The choice was made to pull all capsules off the shelves,

1. The following story is recited in Al Gini and Ronald M. Green's book, *10 Virtues of Outstanding Leaders, Leadership and Character* (Oxford & Chichester: Wiley/Blackwell, 2013), pp. 73-79.

2. https://www.jnj.com/tag/our-credo

and examine and restart production. It was financially a very costly decision.[3]

These critical actions carried out with such decisive promptitude, illustrate what we mean by trustworthiness. Meanwhile, other rival companies were taking advantage of such transparency. Three years later a skilled perpetrator once more penetrated a few capsules with cyanide poisoning. One more victim died. Now Burke publicly confessed he wished the company had never used the form of capsules. But he saved the brand by his transparency, and the brand and its product still survive to-day.

We therefore ask, where did Burke ever receive the moral resources for such honesty and courage. He was a Christian! He himself confessed: "I guess partly because of the way I was brought up – I had a set of values that I knew I was going to have difficulties compromising ever. I never had any doubts to speak of about right and wrong because my father had no doubts… My Mother was extraordinarily bright, and loved intellectual ferment. She taught us all to challenge everything. Our dinner table – or every meal – was a constant arguing over anything and everything."[4]

Burke grew up in a rigorous Catholic school, went for a brief stint into the navy, and then proceeded to Harvard Business School. Thus, he grew up and matured, with a rich family nurture, a highly intelligent Christian faith, and with a strong personal discipline. He was well prepared, like a strong cedar of Lebanon, to confront cre-

3. Al Gini and Ronald M. Green, *op. cit.*, p. 76.
4. *Ibid*, p.74.

atively the most critical storm of his life. He wonderfully exemplified good leadership.

The Limits of Leadership

But extraordinary leadership can only go so far. For we tend to assume good leaders or bad leaders have far more power than they do have. The captain of the *Titanic* could only navigate, he could not prevent the huge ship sinking under an ice-floe. What he could control were the multiple choices being made by many other members of his crew, in the differing complex functions of running the ship, as well as the external warning systems.

Two employees of London Underground made choices not to pick up a smoldering rag, and not to set off the alarm signal about the presence of smoke. One or more navigation officers on the bridge of the *Titanic* saw the looming ice-berg, but chose not to alter course, until it was too late. Individual choices then, are far more significant than we often ever realize. Everyone has the obligation to do their part. But if the job-description is not clear enough, if the individual has never been trained and disciplined to behave responsibly, if 'a whole chain of –ifs', are not in place, then inertia rules mightily and at times, disastrously so. It is the lesson of the old nursery rhyme – "for the loss of the nail, the shoe was lost", then the horse was lost, the rider, the battle, and ultimately "the Kingdom was lost".

The Prevailing Climate of Culture

Like the environmental climate, a human culture is a highly intricate system of multifold activities. Since they are human, again they reflect upon multiple decisions and actions of people. The choice of the Age of Reason, was to be and to promote being hyper-cognitive. A strong reaction set in to become various Romantic cultures. Now in Post-Modernism we are choosing to be much more emotionally intelligent, and gain even spiritual intelligence. This we have described before. We are habituated by culture, as well as inhibited by it. It is therefore the hardest change to make.

But again a strong and intelligent leader can guide us into the creation of a new culture. Soren Kierkegaard laid the foundations, with his protest against nominalism within Christendom. But John MacMurray(1891-1976), in association with others, that he was unaware of, like Emmanuel Mounier in France, then Jacques Ellul, and later French Christian philosophers beyond his time, such Paul Ricoeur, who introduced us into the shaping of a much more "personal" culture.

Tony Blair, the former British Prime Minister was taught by MacMurray at Balliol College, Oxford. His influence over Blair was life-long, explaining the "new Socialism" Blair introduced into British politics. It was

MacMurray who offered two insights. Firstly, he places the individual firmly within a social setting. We are *what* and *who* we are, in part because of the other, the 'You' and "I". Secondly, by rooting his vision in the personal world, he rejects simple determinism. The personal is not submerged in the social nor in the organic model. That is why so many business models are still too abstract, whether it be theoretical models, or even ecosystems. Whether it be intelligent, emotional, spiritual, or even Christian, it must be based in this world of space and time.

The persuasive power of MacMurray was that, as A.R. Duncan has put it, "he chose to think philosophically about problems which seemed to him to arise directly out of the life of the society in which he found himself living."[5] At the same time, MacMurray once remarked, that if he were to live to 105 when his Mother died, he probably would not even then, have persuaded a single professional philosopher. With such radicalism against the culture, MacMurray had Marxist sympathies for the same radical spirit he shared with Karl Marx against Victorian capitalism. The difference with Karl Marx was that 'personalism' is intrinsically humane, while Marxism proved to be deadly.

In his maturity, and now a Quaker, living in a Quaker community, he sought a form of Christianity that was free from nationalism, as in our state churches, and from dogma without life. In his Gifford lectures of 1957,

5. A.R. Duncan, *On the Nature of Persons* (New York: Peter Lang, 1990), p.2.

he wrote, "All meaningful knowledge is for the sake of action, and all meaningful action is for the sake of friendship."[6] Emmanuel Mounier who followed MacMurray, literally poured out his life, dying earlier, for the passion of the creation in France of a 'personalist' culture. As he said:

> If there is one affirmation that is common to all Personalist Philosophies...it is that the basic impulse of persons is not in the isolated perception of the self (cogito) nor the egocentric concern for self, but the communication of consciousness...the adult only finds himself in relationship to others and to things, in work and comradeship, in friendship and in love, in action and encounter, and not in his relationship to himself.[7]

The parallels with MacMurray are clear. But as I shared in an address to the Canadian Christian Council for Higher Education some time ago, the Christian lineage of Personalism is complex but sourced in Hammell, the antagonist friend of Immanuel Kant, flowing through Soren Kierkegaard, and with several tributaries since then.

Living and being renewed daily in the personalist environment of being a "self-for-the-other," requires the

6. John MacMurray, *The Self as Agent* (London: Faber & Faber, 1957), p. 15.

7. Emmanuel Mounier, *Be Not Afraid* (London: Rockliff, 1951), p. 176.

constant self-realization of, "who am I?" As MacMurray himself said,

"For to realize ourselves requires us to be ourselves, to make ourselves real. That means thinking, and feeling really, for ourselves, and expressing this reality in word and action. And this is freedom, and the secret of it lies in our capacity for friendship."[8]

The Nature of True Authority

Authority has a broad spectrum, between the exercise of power and the exercise of legitimacy. Power is required when legitimacy is weak. As the may preacher put in his sermon notes, "argument weak, shout out." This is no different from the authoritarian governments of dictators, who have to exercise more and more power, as the legitimacy of their governance becomes weaker and weaker, and the more they want to hold on to power. *Vox populi*, it is the voice of the people that has legitimacy, as every effort to sustain true democracy is well known in the practice of political science. Then with high legitimacy there is low exercise of power, other than to resist the corruption of legitimacy, whether it be in the voting system or in the sustainment of governance more broadly.

It is no different in business. As we have just seen in the previous chapters, the view of the Promised Land is where Moses united the people by the Ten Commandments, to

8. John MacMurray, *Freedom in the Modern World* (London: Faber & Faber, 1932; New Jersey: Humanities Press, 1991), p. 218.

have a united voice in a united community. This too, is the premise of a company carrying out its business. There is the united voice of the whole organization, not just the voice of the boss. Her leadership is tested for legitimacy according to whether it is the shared voice of the organization, or only one opinion. The health and sustainability of an organization is all grounded upon its legitimacy.

A Thought on Changing Culture

In order to change, new choices have to be made, and many are big and painful, like cutting budgets or investing in a new innovation with significant risk. New imagination is required to see things differently, to re-appreciate the company's future markets. New organization may be needed, as the old practices have not worked. These things are all significant!

But even the smallest of choices matter too. As a Scot, I think of an amusing example. Dundee is famed for its marmalade orange preserve, still exported throughout the old British empire. Part of this old colonial culture is to have marmalade for breakfast. How did all this begin?

With the wreckage of the Spanish Armada in 1492, by storms off the coasts of Britain, one ship sunk off the coast of the Firth of Forth, sending a floating 'armada' of Seville/bitter oranges onshore. They were inedible! But a thrifty housewife picked them up from the shore, boiled them with sugar and created orange marmalade! One simple choice created an international business and the culture of the British empire! As every Brit knows: you cannot have breakfast without orange marmalade!

To pick up again on the metaphor of breakfast in a different way, Peter Drucker, the father of modern management, is famous for having said: "Culture eats strategy for breakfast."[9]

Why is the culture of a business so crucial? For what is being cultivated is an environment to nurture of every seed in the ground, every person in the company. All of this creates a continuously changing environment or culture in the business. It can never be allowed to stagnate and to become habitual. Good intentions – realized, must rule, not inertia. For it is not words that count, but actions taken.

Questions for Further Reflection

1. Often, we have more opportunity to make choices in situations we face in life and in work than it might first appear. Think back on the last few months some occasions when you have done the right thing simply because it is the right thing to do. Consider how you might build the courage and clarity to make choices like that once more per week, or even once more per day. (FGS p. 64) What would it look like for you to pursue similar resolve in the choices you and your

9. Peter Drucker, "Leadership: More Doing than Dash", *The Wall Street Journal,* Jan. 6, 1988.

colleagues face at work?

2. No one is an island – we all have several communities we are a part of that each have distinct culture. How might you be uniquely placed to help change for the better the various "cultures" you participate in shaping?

3. What "cascade movements" (where every member of a community makes small intentional decisions - FGS p. 64) have Christians precipitated in the past that have impacted cultures? What are some we might be called to pursue in the broader context?

4. Think back on a time when someone you know "embodied" (FGS p. 68) a quality or reality that they aspired to, and in doing so made that aspiration – in that instance, real? Consider asking them about the occasion. What did they find difficult, easy, and learn?

5. Consider opportunities you might have to embody something you aspire to and imagine how you might act should those opportunities present themselves.

7

Embodying Godly Leadership

A purposeful enterprise begins with you and me, as we ask ourselves "who am I?" Of course, the reaction of colleagues, when something radically new is being proposed, is to lay down the challenge to one's authority and personhood, "Who do think you are?" Their reaction may be legitimate to ask for evidence of authority if I am acting in an authoritarian or unorthodox way as I propose something new. It was no different with the reaction of the Scribes and the Pharisees to the drastic actions of Jesus, as they asked him: "Tell us, by what authority you are doing these things...who gave you this authority?" while he cleansed the temple court-yard of the greedy traders who exploited the piety of the worshippers and his Father's house (Lk. 20:1-2).

American culture is saturated with the cult of leadership, so that political elections are penalizing its spirit of democracy. Sell "Leadership" magazine in Australia, and your future will be out on the street. For as the Aussies like to say, "they cut down tall poppies." We Canadians are more cynical about a leadership culture. It is a healthier society when we have to see the critical evidence for the qualities of leadership. Otherwise we get the leaders we deserve; poor discernment generates poor choices.

What none of us are good at asking, however is the question of Rob Goffee and Gareth Jones, *Why Should Anyone be Led by You?* The criteria, following the Biblical story of the Children of Israel is all about what Moses was doing. Then what are the ten commandments of leadership that Moses would bring us from Mount Sinai? What are those two tablets of stone? They are like the Lord's Prayer. On the first tablet we have the first four commandments, as in the Lord's Prayer we have the first three petitions, both authorizing, "Let God be God". Then on the second tablet, we have the next six commandments, demanding 'let Man be a genuine human being'; as the last four petitions of the Lord's Prayer re-iterate.

How then can we describe the traits of a Godly leader, whether in the community, the church or a business?

A Godly Leader Has Moral Vision

Moses ascended the Mountain to have a vision of God. Sinners, as we all are, never see God, as Moses was told, "You cannot see my face, for no one may see God and live". (Ex. 33:20). Instead, Moses was assured God would protect him, by hiding Him in the cleft of the rock. (v. 22) Visionary leaders are given wide perspectives that make them safely wise leaders, because they can see 'the whole picture, or the situation' they are in, free from fear i.e. 'hiding in the cleft of the rock'.

The Greeks called this the ability to have good practical reasoning and judgment, *phronesis*, as a necessary part of *moral vision*. But it requires more, in having the need also of *moral wisdom*. This implies the implementation of *moral knowledge*.

It is like being a navigator, skilled in using a compass. It is exemplified by leaders "called for the hour" like Abraham Lincoln, Winston Churchill, and Martin Luther King, being prepared like Moses, by a long tutelage of long hardships, frustrations, and social hiddenness, to then stand, calling, "Let my People be Set Free."

A Godly Leader Is Deeply Selfless

For Christ is our sacrifice; we dwell within His action, and when we are called to sacrifice we imitate the suffering of God. Rare are such leaders, though we can cite Mahatma Gandhi and Nelson Mandela. In the business, we can think of Lee Iacocca, whose company Chrysler faced bankruptcy in the 1970's. Facing this prospect, he reduced his annual salary to one dollar.

What this shows is that major crises demand superior leadership, which demand superior personal sacrifices. Such leaders are models to the people who follow them and invite imitation of their example. But there is also the clear promise, "we can do it", provided there is total transparency, and full embodiment of all that is needed. This is how our way of life may be Godly and wise, whether in the church or in the business world.

A Godly Leader Is a Truth Teller

Christ has proclaimed, "I am the Way, the Truth and the Life." Any other way is falling into darkness. This is still illustrated in so much bureaucracy, reflected in the confusion of wandering between management and the rules! Moses witnessed God parting a miraculous way through the Red Sea! A good leader does the same, in this analogy. He opens a "way" through the confusion of the procedural, or of abstract rules and regulations. He does so transparently.

But lying and deception are two of the worst consequences for an organization, as our judicial system still condemns so consistently. A company can never survive these vices. Deceit is more guileful, and the cover-ups that are practiced eventually become the undoing of a corporation. A good therapy then, for exercising transparency, is always asking the question 'why'. Often women are very good at asking this probing question, since perhaps until recently their voices have not been heard in chauvinistic cultures. So listen now to their voices in the company!

It is significant that we cannot cite conspicuous leaders who are truth tellers, because it is needed at such simple levels of life. Yet it is so profoundly necessary from all of us, to become even more transparent through continual exercise of truthfulness!

A Godly Leader Shows Compassionate Love

Again, this goes way beyond what a secular culture expects of its business leaders. Yet they hunger for it, never having enough of its virtue. Practically, it is what resonates within the needs of their followers. Cohesion is given to the team, when they can both give and receive it.

As the Latin spells it out, *cum ('with')* and the verb *patiscor* ('to suffer') is further enriched by such 'suffering coming from/ or with the heart'. Synonyms like empathy, sympathy, kindness, attention, all play their part in the appeal of compassionate leadership. Again, women, more than men seem to excel in this virtue, yet they have played a lesser role in business. So we welcome the increased role of female leadership that is now taking place, which enriches corporate life, as indeed church life.

But compassion is also a highly ambiguous virtue, when we think of the tragedies of cult leaders like Jim Jones or David Koresh, seducing their needy followers into a death-trap. If 'compassion' is not motivated by *agape* or Christian love, charismatic love can be deadly indeed! *Agape* must rule, not *charism*! Charismatic leadership can become very dangerous, as the twentieth century has so tragically demonstrated.

The whole theme of *For Goodness' Sake*, is about becoming a "self-for-the-other". This so easily gets lost in a bureaucratic organization. A horrific example was the outbreak of the devastating fire that broke out in the London Underground transit system at one of the main hubs of the system, King's Cross. More than a quarter million commuters pass through its six different train lines. It was a November evening of 1987, when Philip Bricknell was collecting train tickets. A commuter stopped him, and said there was a burning tissue at the bottom of one of the longest escalators, servicing the Piccadily line. He went, and with a rolled-up magazine thought he had put out the fire. But it was not his business to do this, nor to report it to the Fire Department.

For decades, four Barons had ruled the tightly run system of 19,000 employees: civil, signal, electrical and mechanical engineering. Even at the highest level, no one was likely to trespass on the territory of another. But fifteen minutes after Bricknell returned to his booth, Christopher Haze, the safety inspector was aroused by two different commuters, one who saw a wisp of smoke, and another who then saw smoke and glow. He hit an emergency button, shouting to fellow commuters to run for it. Yet Haze still did nothing, for he had not seen the smoke himself, and it was an unwritten rule, never to call the fire department unless absolutely necessary. Almost half an hour after the burning tissue was first noticed, the underground was on fire, each arriving train bringing great gusts of new air to fuel the blazing fire.

Thirty-one people died, and many more suffered injuries. The impeccable routines of London Underground's system, the rigid job-descriptions and responsibilities all suddenly became very dangerous. Twenty years' worth of old paint layered throughout the underground could be a fire hazard, the director of operations had once observed. But it was not his department, as the director of maintenance had told him savagely; causing him to withdraw his report.

Further delays occurred with the bureaucratic organization of the fire department, whose dozens of fire trucks were waiting outside the station, which was already in a blaze of fire with explosions. For the firemen were forbidden from using the hydrants of the Underground, only those outside. Thus, it took a total of six hours from when the burning tissue was first reported until the blaze was finally under control. "It's none of your business," and, "that's not my responsibility," had become a great saga of tragedy for London Underground. It took a further year for the commissioner of enquiry to break through the whole bureaucratic culture of London Underground. For he was continually blocked by the unrepentant bureaucratic leaders. The lesson is still in the making, that some things are everyone's business![1] This we can call compassion.

A Godly Leader Is Peaceable

This brings health to an organization, as *shalom* did for

1. Charles Duhigg, *The Power of Habit: Why We Do What We Do in Life and Business* (New York: Random House, 2014), pp.161-73.

Israel. As a leader of peace, a Godly leader avoids unnecessary conflict in the organization, because peace is embodied in his/her inner life. The practice of the Jewish Sabbath was not just a cultural identity of being Jewish, it was intended to be a personal identity of each Israelite. Likewise, Christians need to bear a "sabbath identity," not just in Sunday observance, now the first day of the week, but in being personally "in Christ," where peace eternally dwells. Then when our own heart is at peace, we have the resources to radiate peace around us, for we are always living in the presence of the Lord. Others then see we have a redemptive, radiating presence that provides and blesses others with peace.

This is not taught in business ethics, but a Christian leader learns it in the school of Christ. For the blessed invitation, when accepted, brings *shalom*.

"Come unto me, all who labor and are heavy laden, and I will give you rest. Take my yoke upon you and learn of Me. For my yoke is easy, my burden is light." (Matt. 11:28)

No doubt there were hearers who wondered what this yoke was. For as a youth, Jesus worked as a carpenter with his earthly father, Joseph. He perhaps learnt to make good, reliable yokes, for his peasant customers, to plough the land. Such simple diligence, was no different from what Jesus was acting out in his divine Sonship, being both human and divine.

A Godly Leader Is Trustworthy

Moral consistency is essential in all walks of life, whatever the issue happens to be. In a recent homily, Pope Francis said recently: "an atheist is morally more consistent than 'a sacramental Catholic' who performs religiously all the sacramental life, yet he exploits his employees in business, does money laundering, etc."[2] Of course, it is very difficult to have moral coherence.

Even our secular colleagues are aware that if an executive is having 'an affair', and hiding it, how trustworthy can such a colleague be in the business community. Lying does not stop with one relationship! Deception in all its forms and tendencies should be abhorred. It is a form of stealing, as well as lying. Yet this is being practiced so often, simply because people have a low self-image that goes with emotional insecurity. Basically, it is the fear of facing reality, and therefore the truth about themselves. Yet it is the source of so much bureaucratic practice and of cultural compliance.

It can take great courage then, to "stand up and be counted." It is illustrated existentially, to exist like Kierkegaard's lonely individual, the "I" against the whole system/culture. Soren Kierkegaard, known as "the Father of Existentialism" stood out like one solitary fir tree, verti-

2. *The National Post, Friday Feb. 24, 2017, pp. A1-2.*

cal upon the horizontal landscape of the Jutland heath. In his day, there was a cultural mandate known as the law of Jante: "thou shalt not be different from anybody else." This culture he sought to shatter, step by step.

But an insecure identity dares not stand out. Yet such a weak identity constantly creates havoc wherever it prevails over a community. It is also always pretending and lying, and lying especially is instrumental in all wrongdoing, small or big. It is needed to manipulate public opinion in one's favor.

It is difficult to point out the deception of a leader in a dishonest system. One can become conditioned to certain behavior, as the Nazi followers were blinded from recognizing their complicity with evil and instead believed they were simply being good citizens. Nazi acolytes were thus terribly blinded by their culture of unexamined obedience, literally of 'listening to ' (Latin *ob audire*) the flood of orders given them by a totalitarian regime. Yet it is no different from any bureaucratic form of governance. Which is why a politician may forfeit his/her role in the cabinet, or indeed as a church leader, by choosing to remain morally consistent, and thus trustworthy, even if it requires them to stand out like Kierkegaard.

Trustworthiness therefore requires moral courage, for whatever reason: for fear of criticism; for loss of popularity; for fear of being misunderstood; for even the fear of losing one's job.

A Godly Leader Is Not Envious

Envy is the twin of pride, the most persuasive of all sins. It blinds us to see the good qualities of "the other", and therefore it precludes a person from good judgment about one's own colleagues, for co-operative action. Instead, it isolates a person in selfishness, undermining the good qualities one may otherwise have. In its pervasiveness, Rene Gerard has demonstrated so clearly, envy is the original source of all human culture!

Envy is the inordinate desire for that which belongs to others, so it is a form of social theft. Yet it is not just about wanting what others possess, be it status, money, talents, or good looks. In anger and frustration, envy can ultimately say, "I want your life!" It is an anti-rational sentiment that can become socially dangerous, in diminishing fairness and social justice. In a work-force, it can create havoc.

For if anything is needed of social justice in a work-force, it is impartiality. And the ability to overcome all sorts of prejudice, whether of ethnic race and color, religion, or personality. For envy is a form of rancor that hurts everyone, the envious included!

The Godly Leader that is not envious must have moral courage, as all other virtues require. He/she needs also to be selfless. Both of these values then interlock into a relational whole, for a leader to be a good person. In an increasingly individualistic society, as we have previously seen, ethical values, rather than social morality, must prevail.

***

Embodiment is the summary of Good Leadership, as it is of Good Business. It is climactic, like entering into the Promised Land. It has to face the daily challenge of "why should anyone be led by you?"[3] As *For Goodness' Sake* puts it: "The underlying assumption is that leadership is something we do *to* other people. But in our view, leadership should be seen as something we do *with* other people."[4] This does not come with giving good advice, but by the exemplary *being and embodiment* of the leader(s).

Questions for Further Reflection

1. This is one lens for looking at Godly leadership – how does it fit with your own mental models (or others you have encountered) around what it takes to be a Godly leader? What did you find helpful? What would you add?

2. What people in your life do you feel you are called to "do leadership" **with**? How are you connecting with

3. Rob Goffee and Gareth Jones, *Why Should Anyone be Led by You?* (Boston: Harvard Business Review Press, 2006).

4. *For Goodness' Sake*, p. 69.

them intentionally to pursue that call together?

3. How do you think exploration of the disciples and the early church might help Christians understand the concept of leadership and embodiment (FGS p. 70) more fully?

Conclusion

The "golden thread" that Ariadne spun in the classical myth is sustainability. To escape from the labyrinth of mindless bureaucracy, corruption, and many other institutional evils, we have constantly to ask what will keep us sustainable. Of course, it has to be the truth, transparency and humility, in exposing corruption and fraud, social injustice, and may other evils.

Yet none of us are perfect, and no one has all the virtues needed for co-operative existence together. We will always need each other, for there will always be a host of little and big things that need attention. We will always be re-shaping, re-forming, and exercising many other "re's". But first, we all need *metanoia*, to be emancipated ourselves and to help emancipate others, from the *status quo*.

The Theological Virtues of Faith, Hope, and Love

In the theological virtues of faith, hope, and love, the Christian business leader, like all Christians, has the privilege of exercising the power of transcendence.

Thinking in faith means praying, so the more we pray over our company affairs, as we pray for our family life, the more our perception is enlarged; we are given much broader and deeper vision.

In turn, praying means living attentively to all the needs around us. Such moral "attention-paying", makes us more aware of the vigilance we need to the presence and threat of evil in all its subtle manifestations, all around us. Prayer makes us become more God-conscious, rather than remaining merely self-conscious. Once again, all this reinforces sobriety and humility. Faith in action then becomes far more than doctrinal assent, any more than it is merely giving assent to the mission statement of a company.

The virtue of hope means transcending our present circumstances. Jurgen Moltmann is a great contemporary theologian of hope.[1] His first book on *The Theology of Hope* was written over fifty years ago, and since his own youthful experience of war-time imprisonment, he has been an exemplar of Christian hope ever since. In the flow of history there is no prospect that we shall have better times in future. It is in being emancipated from the time process, to have hope in the Kingdom of God, that we have a leverage to lift us to another realm of thinking and being. The hope of the Christian does not lie in this world, although it can profoundly bless this world, if we act as

1. Jurgen Moltmann, *The Living God and the Fullness of Life* (Louisville, KY: Westminster John Knox Press, 2015).

its agents, secretive as we may need to be, for our message to be accepted. This was the great ploy of Malcolm Muggeridge, as a late convert to Christianity, and having served in the secret service in World War II. He had become "a stay-behind agent" for God's Kingdom.

We are never paralyzed by the *status quo*, when we have hope, for we are always reaching forward. As Isaiah 43:18,19 puts it:

> Do not remember the former things
> or consider the things of old.
> I am about to do a new thing;
> Now it springs forth, do you not perceive it?

Each day she goes to work, the hopeful Christian leader looks to see what "new thing" God will enable her to see. Such is the transcendent virtue of hope, in its imminence for today. We think it is all about *chronos* – time measured by the clock, to discover it is all about *kairos* –transformative time taking us into a wholly different realm.[2]

Being hopeful in our thinking then, is first of all *to think of past memories*, to rediscover past solutions, to reflect on missed opportunities, to see what can still be resolved. Secondly, hoping is *anticipation,* in awareness of new possibilities, remembering all the "re-" of our past cultural history: Re-naissance, Re-formation, Re-volution, all in the hope of re-newal, even re-birth. Thirdly, hoping is *imagining*, producing images of the future we would de-

2. See the Samuel Beckett's play, *Waiting for Godot,* for the tension he builds between *chronos* and *kairos*.

sire to be re-created. It is what Kant called, "the transcendental power of the imagination."

Love, as the third theological virtue, has been perhaps most profoundly explored in the twentieth century by the Catholic philosopher, Dietrich von Hildebrand (1889-1977). Like Augustine, late in life, he began around 1958 to pioneer thinking around an expression of love as unification.[3] Applied at work, qualities that promote unification such as sympathy and kindness can be proactive expressions of love. von Hildebrand, it seems, might suggest that to love one's colleagues also involves generating an environment of unity, of mutual appreciation of each other, and indeed in taking an affective delight in each other.

We all know of the deep need all humans have to be loved and to love. Von Hildebrand was conscious that we live in a realm of values, values which envelop us all the time. To him the third component of the triad of love, is then value –response.[4] We love what we appreciate and value. I am empowered also to love the other, as I am myself the recipient of love, since even selflessness can be neurotic. All this is played out every day in the office!

Questions for Further Reflection

1. In what ways are Christ-followers naturally non-con-

3. Dietrich von Hildebrand, *The Nature of Love,* trans. by John F. Crosby with John Henry Crosby (South Bend, Indiana: St. Augustine's Press, 2009).

4. *Ibid,* pp. 15-40

formers (FGS p. 85) and how does this help us lead out with courage and humility as an example for others? In what ways should we as Christ-followers be non-conformers but tend to fall short?

2. Consider growing your moral "attention-paying" by asking God to help you become more "God-conscious" to hear His voice each day in the places to which He has called you.

3. What might the Lord be saying to you, now, in the places you are in?

4. What acts of faith, hope and love – small, large, and in-between – is Jesus inviting you into as He brings His Kingdom? What resources in the places you find yourself – both "secular" and "sacred" – might be of use to Him in that great restoration project the Holy Spirit invites us to participate in?

Bibliography

Anderson, J.R.L. *The Ulysses Factor: The Exploring Instinct in Man*. London: Houghton & Stoughton, 1970.

Barth, Hans-Martin. *The Theology of Martin Luther*. Minneapolis: Fortress Press, 2009.

Bowra, C.M. *The Greek Experience*. London: Weidenfeld and Nicolson, 1959.

Carpenter, R.S. "Ecosystem Ecology', in *Ecology*, edit. S. I. Dodson, *et al*. New York: Oxford University Press, 1998.

Coghill, Nevill. *Visions from Piers Plowman, A New Rendering of Langland's Original*. New York: Oxford University Press, 1970.

Colson, Charles W. *Born Again*. Old Tappan, New Jersey: Chosen Books, 1976.

Downs, David. "Paul's Collection and the Book of Acts Revisited." *New Testament Studies*. Volume 52(1), 50-70. Cambridge: Cambridge University Press, 2006.

Drucker, Peter. "Leadership: More Doing than Dash", *The Wall Street Journal*. Jan. 6, 1988.

Duhigg, Charles. *The Power of Habit: Why We Do What We Do in Life and Business*. New York: Random House, 2014.

Duncan, A.R. *On the Nature of Persons*. New York: Peter Lang, 1990.

Gay, Craig M. *The Way of the (Modern) World, or Why it's Tempting to Live as if God Doesn't Exist.* Grand Rapids, MI: Wm. B. Eerdmans, 1998.

Gini, Al and Ronald M. Green. *10 Virtues of Outstanding Leaders, Leadership and Character.* Oxford & Chichester: Wiley/Blackwell, 2013.

Goffee, Rob and Gareth Jones. *Why Should Anyone be Led by You?* Boston: Harvard Business Review Press, 2006.

Gunderson, Lance H. and C.S. Holling, edit. *Panarchy: Understanding Transformations in Human and Natural Systems.* Washington DC: Island Press, 2002.

Heidl, Stefan. *Philosophical Problems of Behavioural Economics.* London: Routledge, 2016.

Houston, Christopher. *For Goodness' Sake: Satisfy the Hunger for Meaningful Business.* Moffat, Ontario: Change Alliance, 2017.

Hughes, J.D. edit. "Pan: Environmental Crisis in Classical Polytheism" in *Religion and Environmental Crisis.* Athens, GA: University of Georgia Press, 1986.

Hurst, David. *The New Ecology of Leadership: Business Mastery in a Chaotic World.* New York: Columbia University Press, 2012.

Inrig, Gary. *Your Money Matters: Financial Wisdom from the Parables of Jesus.* Grand Rapids, MI: Discovery House Publishers, 2014.

Lang, Amanda. *The Power of Why.* Toronto: Harper Collins, 2012.

MacMurray, John. *Freedom in the Modern World.* London: Faber & Faber, 1932; New Jersey: Humanities Press, 1991.

MacMurray, John. *The Self as Agent.* London: Faber & Faber, 1957.

Martin, Vibeke Norgaard with Matthew Frederick. *101 Things I Learned in Law School.* New York: Grand Central, 2013.

Moltmann, Jurgen. *The Living God and the Fullness of Life.* Louisville, KY: Westminster John Knox Press, 2015.

Mounier, Emmanuel. *Be Not Afraid.* London: Rockliff, 1951.

Mourkogiannis, Nikos. *PURPOSE: the Starting Point of Great Companies.* New York: St.Martin's Press, 2006.

Murdoch, Iris. *The Sovereignty of Good Over Other Concepts.* Cambridge: Cambridge University Press, 1967.

Simmel, Georg. *On Individuality and Social Forms,* edit. Donald N. Levine. Chicago: The University of Chicago Press, 1971.

Sinek, Simon. *Start with Why: How Great Leaders inspire Everyone to Take Action.* New York: Portfolio Penguin, 2009.

St. Augustine. *The Trinity.* trans. Edmund Hill O.P. Brooklyn: New City Press, 1991.

St. Augustine. *Tractate 26 on the Gospel of St. John.*

Taylor, Charles. *The Malaise of Modernity.* CBC Massey Lectures, Toronto, 1991.

Tinder, Glenn. *Can We Be Good Without God? On the Political Meaning of Christianity.* Regent College Reprints: Vancouver, 1993.

Torrance, T.F. *Theology in Reconstruction.* Eugene, OR: Wipf & Stock, 1996.

Torrance, T. F. "The Christ Who Loves Us", in *A Passion For Christ: The Vision That Ignites Us.* edit. Thomas F. Torrance, James B. Torrance, David W. Torrance. Edinburgh: The Handsel Press, and PLC Publications, 1999.

Venema, Henry Isaac. *Identifying Selfhood: Imagination, Narrative, and Hermeneutics in the Thought of Paul Ricoeur.* Albany, NY: State University of New York Press, 2000.

Verbrugge, Verlyn D. & Keith R. Krell. *Paul & Money: a Biblical and Theological Analysis of the Apostle's Teachings and Practices*. Grand Rapids, MI: Zondervan, 2015.

von Hagan, Jurgen and Michael Welker. *Money as God: The Monetization of the Market and its Impact on Religion, Politics, Law, and Ethics*. Cambridge: Cambridge University Press, 2014.

von Hildebrand, Dietrich. *The Nature of Love*. trans. by John F. Crosby with John Henry Crosby. South Bend, Indiana: St. Augustine's Press, 2009.

Witherington, Ben. *Friendship and Finances in Philippi*. Valley Forge, PA: Trinity Press International, 1994.

Witherington, Ben. *Jesus and Money: a Guide for Times of Financial Crisis*. Grand Rapids, MI: Baker, 2010.